Imagine a world without you

Poems of personal love and loss
illustrated by uplifting photos

by

Anne Pincombe

Copyright © Anne Pincombe 2021

All rights reserved. No part of this publication may be reproduced, stored in any form of retrieval system or transmitted in any form or by any means without prior permission in writing from the publisher except for the use of brief quotations in a book review.

Table of Contents

Shifting sands	7
The epiphany	10
Imagine	13
Flight	15
How long will it take	17
In memory of my valentine	19
The voice	20
I miss you more and more	23
The streets of freedom	25
Dancing with the angels	27
A sea of faces	29
I wanted to grow old with you	30
How I wonder where you are	33
I've lost the very best of me	34
I'll never forget	37
Time, it marches on	39
Seize the night	41
You and me	43
Haven't seen you for a while	44
Isabella plantation	47
Memories	48
Home alone	51
There'll never be a man like you	55
The kiss	57
The tree of life	59

I have produced this book as a legacy to my husband, George Moutoussis, known to most people as Yogi. Although the poems are personal to me, I hope they may resonate and help bring comfort to anyone who has lost someone they love.

Our story

Every story has a beginning, a middle and an end. Sadly, for us, the end came too soon.

My husband, Yogi, loved life – and he loved people. He would do anything for anyone. We were together for over 25 wonderful years which we lived to the full, and I have beautiful memories that will stay with me forever.

When Yogi was diagnosed with Parkinson's some years ago he didn't let it define him. He carried on working for as long as he could and ultimately we bought a second home in Panormo, Crete in our beloved Greece. We stayed there whenever possible over the years and we met some very special people who, I know, will be lifelong friends.

Yogi loved photography and wherever he went he nearly always had a camera with him. In the past I had written a lot of poetry, but during my years with Yogi I used to joke that I was too happy and that he'd taken away my creativity, which was at its best during times of sadness.

In the last two years of his life, Yogi's Parkinson's and its complications insidiously took over. One of his great sorrows was that he lost his ability to use his camera. When Yogi died in Crete aged 65 I was heartbroken. My creativity returned in force and the poems in this book wrote themselves. They came to me at any time, day or night.

Each poem is illustrated with a photo or creative image produced by Yogi in happier times. Each image has a personal memory attached to it.

Yogi will always be in my heart.

This book is dedicated to Yogi's mother, Mary and to my ever loving sisters Susan, Wendy and Jane as well as my amazing friends. Your unwavering support has made all the difference.

With special thanks for your invaluable creative input to Jan and to Angela as well as to Kim and the team at Publishing Push.

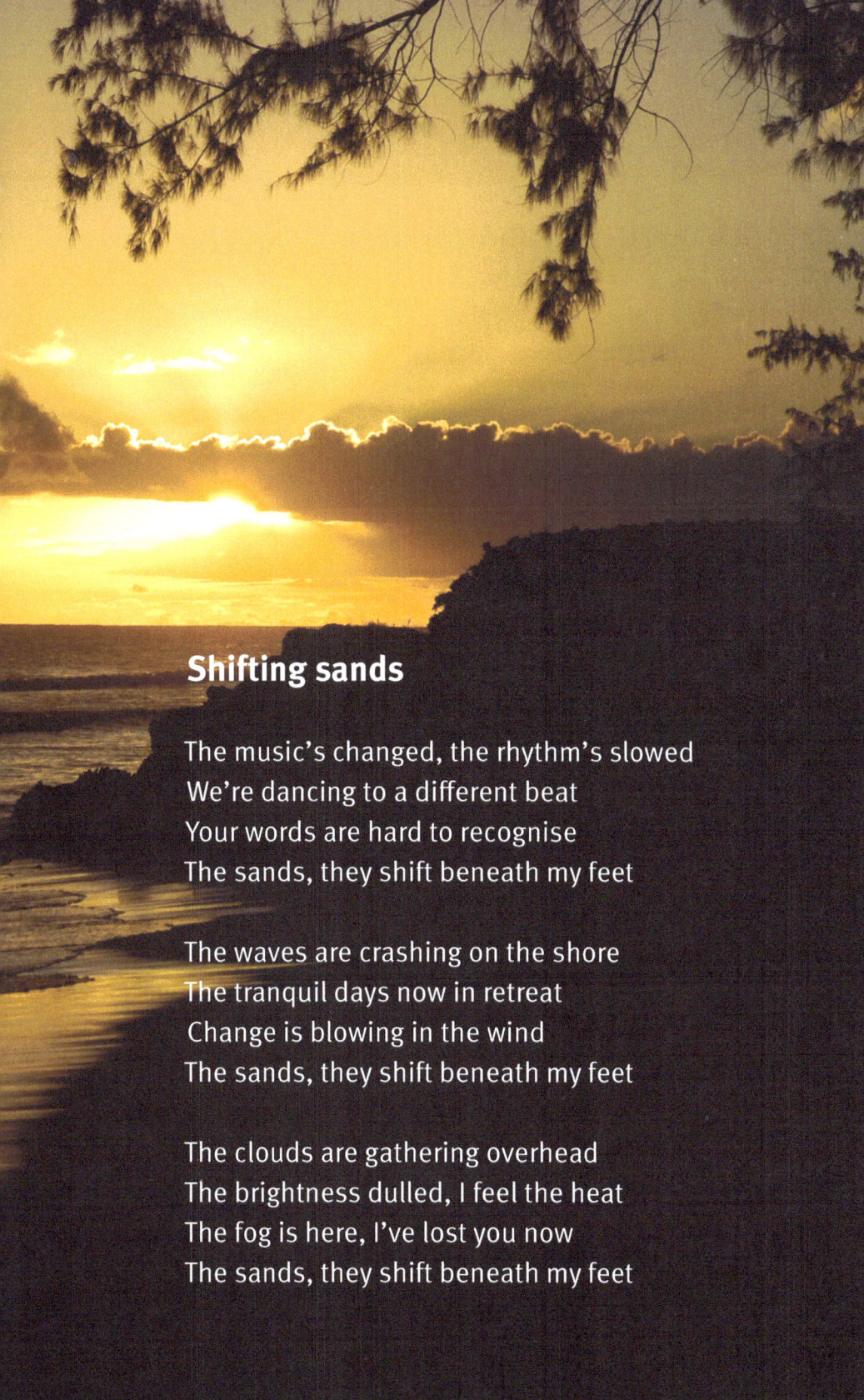

Shifting sands

The music's changed, the rhythm's slowed
We're dancing to a different beat
Your words are hard to recognise
The sands, they shift beneath my feet

The waves are crashing on the shore
The tranquil days now in retreat
Change is blowing in the wind
The sands, they shift beneath my feet

The clouds are gathering overhead
The brightness dulled, I feel the heat
The fog is here, I've lost you now
The sands, they shift beneath my feet

You smile and talk quite normally
The sun returns and life is sweet
Your words they fade and disappear
The sands, they shift beneath my feet

The conversation's muted now
Your memories muddled, on repeat –
Confused by what is going on
The sands, they shift beneath my feet

Your legs they buckle trying to stand
With all your strength you fight defeat
I see your eyes, I feel your pain
The sands, they shift beneath my feet

Your concentration's disappeared
Your sentences are incomplete
Then all at once you're back with me
The sands, they shift beneath my feet

The tide has turned, you're different now
Recuperating here in Crete
Hope's replacing shifting sand
Trickling here beneath my feet

You sleep the sleep of innocence
The nightmares gone, now obsolete
You wake and stretch and look around
The sands feel warm beneath my feet

The shifting sands have turned to grit
There's solid rock there, way down deep
Endurance now will gradually
Expose the ground beneath my feet

Unsteady steps, with rough terrain
Rocky ground, a parapet
But inch by inch, as time goes by
Those shifting sands we will defeat

The epiphany

I set out for that long and distant shore
Unfazed by all that lay along the path
The power of love a constant at my core

But tides can turn at any time of day
The sea of change will rise and fall at will
Exposing all the rocks along the way

The obstacles were soon so plain to see
Retreating seemed the only way to go
I tell myself that what will be will be

We start and stop and start and stop again
We move on forward then go on back once more,
And try hard not to focus on the pain

At times it seems survival is the key
The struggle will be worth it in the end
But the end it is so very hard to see

The wind it raged and howled throughout that night
The rain lashed down with great intensity
Obscuring all that lay within my sight

But come the dawn a peace came over me
The sun returned as night turned into day
And once again the path was clear to see

The shore it still may be just out of sight
But the goal I now know lies within my reach
Time is what we need to make things right

The power of love is conquering and transcending
It will help us move on forward inch by inch
Towards that so elusive happy ending

Imagine

Imagine a sky without any stars
The moon always hidden from view
Imagine the sun without any warmth
Imagine a world without you

Imagine the birds without any song,
The skies always grey, never blue
Imagine a sea that is permanently still
Imagine a world without you

Imagine the earth without any flowers
A vista without any hue
Imagine a landscape that's lifeless and bleak
Imagine a world without you

I've loved you so long and I've loved you so much
That my heart it is broken in two
I'll imagine anything else but I can't
Imagine a world without you

Flight

You always used to wish that you could fly
Rise up and view the world from far above
And now your spirit's soared to unknown heights
Beyond the stars, beyond what we know of

You're now released from all your worldly pain
How wonderful to set your spirit free
No ties on earth to give a blinkered view
To see the world with crystal clarity

I feel you always watching over me
A presence that is much too big to hide
Although you may have gone far far away
I know forever you'll be by my side

How long will it take?

How long will it take till the pain goes away?
I wake and it's here with me, day after day
I can laugh with the best of them, oh, how I've tried
But always, yes always my pain's here inside

So often I've wished I could will it away
But it's obvious to me that it's destined to stay
It's like losing a limb you should no longer feel
The limb may be gone but you still think it's real

I go out to dinner, I'll meet with a friend,
Determined I'll bring all this pain to an end
But the pain it still pulls, although no one can tell
I can laugh even when I am going through hell

And I'm floored by some things that were simple before –
To go to a party and walk through the door,
To join with a group and to talk and to smile –
I can feel so alone, but I'll act all the while

I sit in our home and imagine your touch
You're all I can think of, I miss you so much
I sleep and I dream that you're here by my side
Then I wake and you're gone and the pain's hard to hide

I miss you so much it's a visceral ache
It's an ongoing cycle I can't seem to break
It's a deep rooted pain that just won't go away
I'm resigned to the fact that it's with me to stay

In memory of my valentine

I love you to eternity, I love you to your core,
There's no way in the whole wide world I could have loved you more
You're the man throughout my life I'd always waited for
Always and forever you're the one I will adore

The voice

There's a voice I have inside me
That tells me not to think
To live life in the moment
Not to teeter on the brink

To get up in the mornings
And to focus on a way
To fill my life with things to do
that get me through the day

The night's a different matter
No daytime filter there
I lie awake for hours and hours
The memories, they sear

My friends, they are my lifeline
They know just how I feel
We meet, we talk, we reminisce
My new life is for real

The tears they can surprise me
Coming from, I know not where
One moment I feel happy
The next I feel despair

The cracks can show so easily
The veneer still paper thin
My concentration starts to slip
And you come creeping in

I feel as though my life's on pause,
I'm playing a waiting game
Soon you'll come back home to me
To start our life again

So I'll live life in the moment,
Concentrate on what is real
Some day I may feel different
But I fear my heart won't heal

I miss you more and more

My life is now a parody
Of what we had before
You fill my head, you fill my heart
I miss you more and more

The streets of freedom

I walk the streets of freedom
No more ties to keep me home
I walk the streets of freedom
Full of crowds, yet so alone

I see you on the pavement
Hear you whisper in my ear
Catch your shadow in the sunlight
Touch your hand but you're not there

I hear you in the distance
Feel your presence next to me
Turn to seek the all elusive
Long for what I know can't be

I walk the streets of freedom
Full of crowds but so alone
I'd give the world to go back to
Those ties that kept me home

Dancing with the angels

If only I'd known just how hard it could be
To love, truly love so your world's in a spin
To capture a dream and to find out it's real
Seize the magic and happiness waiting within

Oh I met you too late and I fell for you hard
Our future was evident right from the start
I would never have left you for you were my life
You changed me forever, took over my heart

You were different from anyone I'd ever met
An alchemist holding the key to my door
Turned my world upside down, showed me how life could be
With fun as the focus and love at the core

The pain when you left was like nothing I'd known
A visceral wrench from the depths of my being
I was blinded by tears and a physical wreck
I've been torn up inside, no idea what I'm doing

Whilst you dance with the angels I'll dance all alone
The chords resonate with your songs left for me
Our life now is over, it cuts like a knife
If only I'd known just how hard love can be

A sea of faces

A sea of faces everywhere
I'll search and search but never find
The one that means the world to me
Forever etched upon my mind

I wanted to grow old with you

I wanted to grow old with you
My love, my darling friend
To be together all our lives
Be with you 'til the end

I wanted to grow old with you
To never, ever part
To lie beside you every night
And hear your beating heart

I wanted to grow old with you
Together, you and me
A bond so strong it couldn't break
Joined for eternity

I wanted to grow old with you
Enjoy a life of leisure
To share the simple joys in life
The ones that you can't measure

I wanted to grow old with you
As soulmates, you and me
Entwined beneath the surface
Like the roots upon a tree

I wanted to grow old with you
To share our lives together
To keep the vows I promised you
Always and forever

I wanted to grow old with you
No fears of being alone
Instead, a gradual slowing down
With you, not on my own

But now for you the clock has stopped
For me time marches on
I wanted to grow old with you
Now you're forever young

And as my twilight years approach
I'll face them all alone
I wanted to grow old with you
But now that future's gone

How I wonder where you are...

Have you come back as a moonbeam?
Or a bright and twinkling star?
Or a dazzling ray of sunlight?
How I wonder where you are

The butterflies surround me
Gently fluttering in the light
The birdsong's like a chorus
Is that you in glorious flight?

Are you soaring with the eagles?
Are you rustling in the trees?
Are you my shadow when I'm walking?
Are you whispering in the breeze?

Are you there when I am dreaming?
Are you with me in the night?
Can you hear me when I call you?
Are you here, just out of sight?

When I watch the golden sun set
Or the ever changing sea
When the wind is gently blowing
Are you there, right next to me?

Have you come back as a moonbeam?
Or a bright and twinkling star?
Or a dazzling ray of sunlight?
How I wonder where you are...

I've lost the very best of me

Sometimes I feel so blind with grief
That I can hardly see
The tears they are incessant
The tears for you and me

Of course I know that you have gone
That you're no longer here
And yet my brain won't recognise
A life without you near

I'd never, ever, known the love
You showed me from the start
I knew that once we'd married
We'd never, ever part

You've always been my soulmate,
Always steadfast by my side
With you I was transparent,
With nothing there to hide

You made me feel so special,
Showed me freedom, made me strong,
Gave me wings and taught me how to fly
With you I did no wrong

I knew we both would never stray
I loved our life together
I only ever wanted you
Always and forever

You conquered so much illness
With such courage and no fear
I thought you'd live for ever,
Cling to all that you held dear

Even at the very end
I never thought you'd go
This was just another setback
Just one more to overthrow

But now you've left me, gone for good
I can't believe the pain
I've lost the very best of me
Won't ever love again

I'll never forget

I'll never forget your body, so strong
Your skin, smooth as satin under my touch
Your hair, ultra soft like the finest of silk
All of you, all of you I love so much

Your eyes, so expressive, so very aware
Your face, oh so handsome, so open and true
Your smile, like a light at the end of the day
My husband, my darling, I love all of you

Your laugh, so infectious, so happy and real
Your heart, oh so huge, full of love to your core
Your voice, just like velvet, so strong and so deep
Never, not ever could I love you more

Your hands so protective, so big and so warm
The way that you stand, oh so straight and so tall
My lover, my soulmate, the man of my dreams
I'll never forget that I once had it all

Time, it marches on

The sun it rises then it sets
The days have come and gone
The weeks turn slowly into months
As time it marches on

The seasons change, the days are short
The nights seem really long
The moon it waxes then it wanes
And time, it marches on

Each anniversary bears a scar
Of memories bygone
The tides they ebb and then they flow
And time, it marches on

'Time is the answer,' they all say
'Acceptance it will come –
Just wait and see, all will be well'
And time still marches on

But some things never seem to change:
The stars we gaze upon;
The vastness of the skies above –
Yet time still marches on

It seems for me time has stood still
The pull of love so strong
I'm left here in a different world
Whilst time, it marches on

Seize the night

Grab the stars and hold them tight
As you soar up in glorious flight
Seize the night along the way
The way you used to seize the day

You and me

Bread and butter
Cake and tea
Fish and chips
You and me

Egg and bacon
Sand and sea
Scones and jam
You and me

Love and marriage
Lock and key
Man and wife
You and me

Broken hearts
Setting free
Shattered dreams
You and me

Haven't seen you for a while...

I know you're here, I feel you here
You haven't gone, you're always near
I hear your voice, I sense your smile
Just haven't seen you for a while

I cook the food you love to eat
I drink red wine, I eat red meat
I play your music, sing your tunes
It's like you're here, outside the room

I lie in bed, turn out the light
Feel your breathing in the night
Smile at you and go to sleep
I feel the vigil you will keep

I dream my dreams, you're often there
Happy times without a care
I wake and find an empty bed
The sadness then, it fills my head

I feel a chill, turn up the heat
We're dancing to a different beat
I'm all alone and you're not there
I'll wait, I'm sure you'll soon be here

You'll come back when the time is right
I know you're here, just out of sight
The memories jostle, fight for space
And once again I see your face

I know you're watching over me
I close my eyes and you I see
But oh, how much I miss our life
The simple joy of man and wife

I know you're here, I feel you here
You haven't gone, you're always near
I hear your voice, I sense your smile
Just haven't seen you for a while...

Isabella plantation

How poignant now to be here in this place
We once presumed to think of as our own
Now all around I see your lovely face
Although I sit reflecting all alone
The beauty of the vast and open sky
The winding paths, the slow meandering streams
The vibrant hues a vision to the eye
Surround me as I'm lost within my dreams
And as I feel your presence up above
My heart is filled with all consuming love

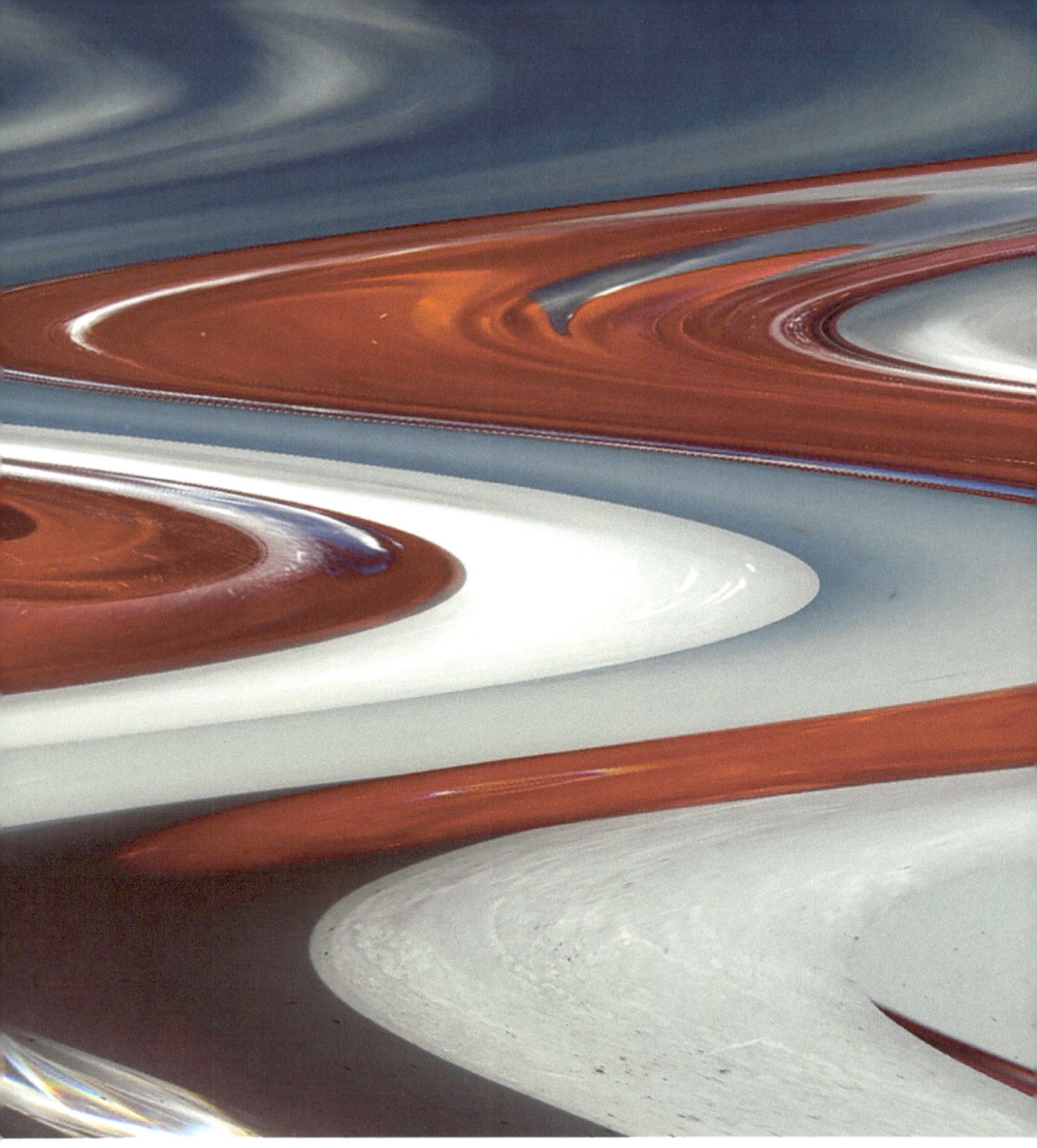

Memories

Somewhere deep inside me
That's hidden far away
I've found a place to keep you
Where my memories won't stray

It's very hard to access
And impossible to see
For no one else can go there
As I hold the only key

But when I'm feeling lonely
And from the world I hide
Sometimes I slowly turn the lock
And venture on inside

My need it overwhelms me
To feel some small relief
From my never ending hunger
The rawness of my grief

Just to see you for a moment
Make believe that you're still here
To alleviate the loneliness
To show how much I care

My mind expands and opens
And the memories crowd in
A kaleidoscope of colour
As the picture shows begin

But soon enough I close the door
Return to what I'm doing
Too long inside that secret place
Will surely be my ruin

Home alone

The saying that your home is where the heart is
Is a saying that I always found so true
Our home was always filled with love and laughter
Reflecting how I spent my life with you

So often you would greet me at our front door
Wait up at night if I was with a friend
I'd always feel so glad to be back with you
Your warmth so welcome at the evening's end

Sometimes you would surprise me with some flowers
A huge bouquet of bright exotic blooms
Not for you the pre packed garage bunches
Like you their presence really filled our rooms

You were such a people person, loved to party
When friends came round you'd come into your own
You'd fill the place with music and with laughter
You loved to welcome people to our home

But some days we would hunker down together
We'd watch TV and cook an easy meal
I'd lie against you, listen to your heart beat
So happy with the way you made me feel

You'd cook me special meals for no real reason
The table laid with candles burning bright
Good music playing softly in the background
You'd make it such a very special night

In summertime you'd go out to the garden
And sometimes choose a perfumed rose for me
You'd put it on a tray with morning coffee
Romantic gestures came so easily

You never were afraid of your emotions
You'd hold my hand and whisper in my ear
You'd stand so tall I'd feel you were my saviour
Wherever I would look I'd find you there

At Christmas you would celebrate for England
With lovely gifts and plentiful champagne
Our table would be filled to overflowing
You really would be king of your domain

You liked to plan surprises for my birthday
It didn't really matter what or where
What mattered was the thought that was behind it
I loved the way you showered me with care

My memories they sometimes overwhelm me
I can see you next to me as clear as day
Feel the love I'd always taken as a given
Not knowing it could ever go away

But now oppressive silence is my welcome
A parody of what I've always known
A bleak reminder of what now lies before me
Of what is now a house, no more a home

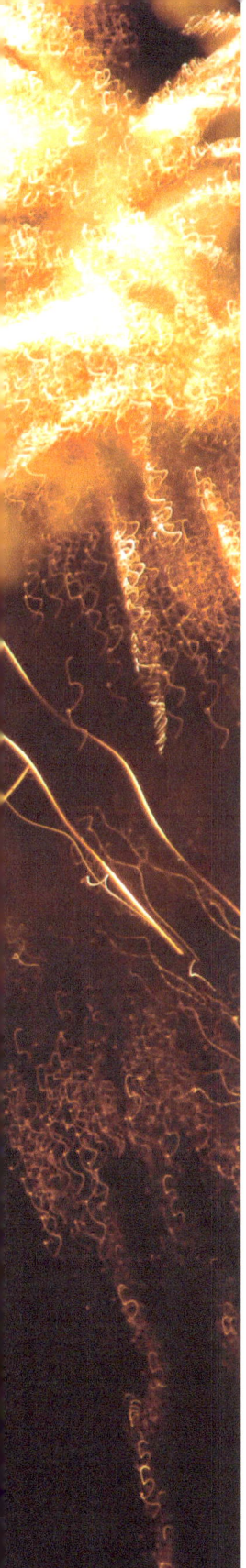

There'll never be a man like you

There'll never be a man like you
You shone so very bright
Your aura was amazing
Surrounding you with light

You drew so many to you
Like a beacon in the room
They were shadows in stark contrast
To your brightness in the gloom

Your energy lit up my life
Your spark has never gone
I feel your presence everywhere
It's here in every room

And when I see the moon at night
It's iridescent beams
The luminescent stars above
I'm lost within my dreams

Your energy is everywhere
I feel it day and night
There'll never be a man like you
You were my guiding light

The kiss

I blow a kiss up to the sky
The wind it takes it, way up high
I never even question why
I know I'll love you till I die

The tree of life

This tree of life's a symbol of
The life you lived so well
The seasons come, the seasons go
The flowers may fade, the leaves
May fall like tears
But the tree will grow
For years and years and years
And bloom and bloom again
Long after we are gone
The memory of its beauty lingering on